This Book belongs To

....

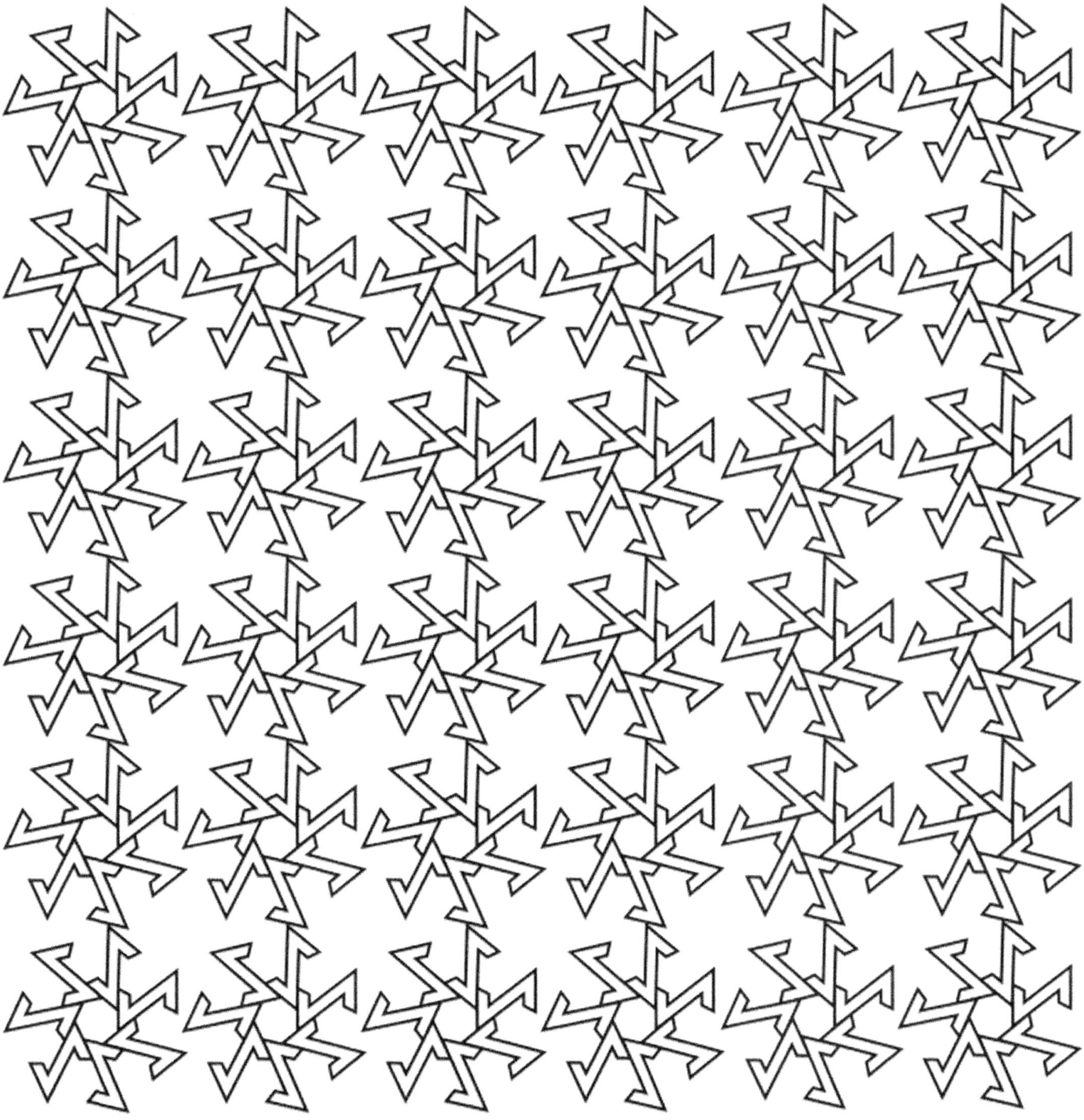

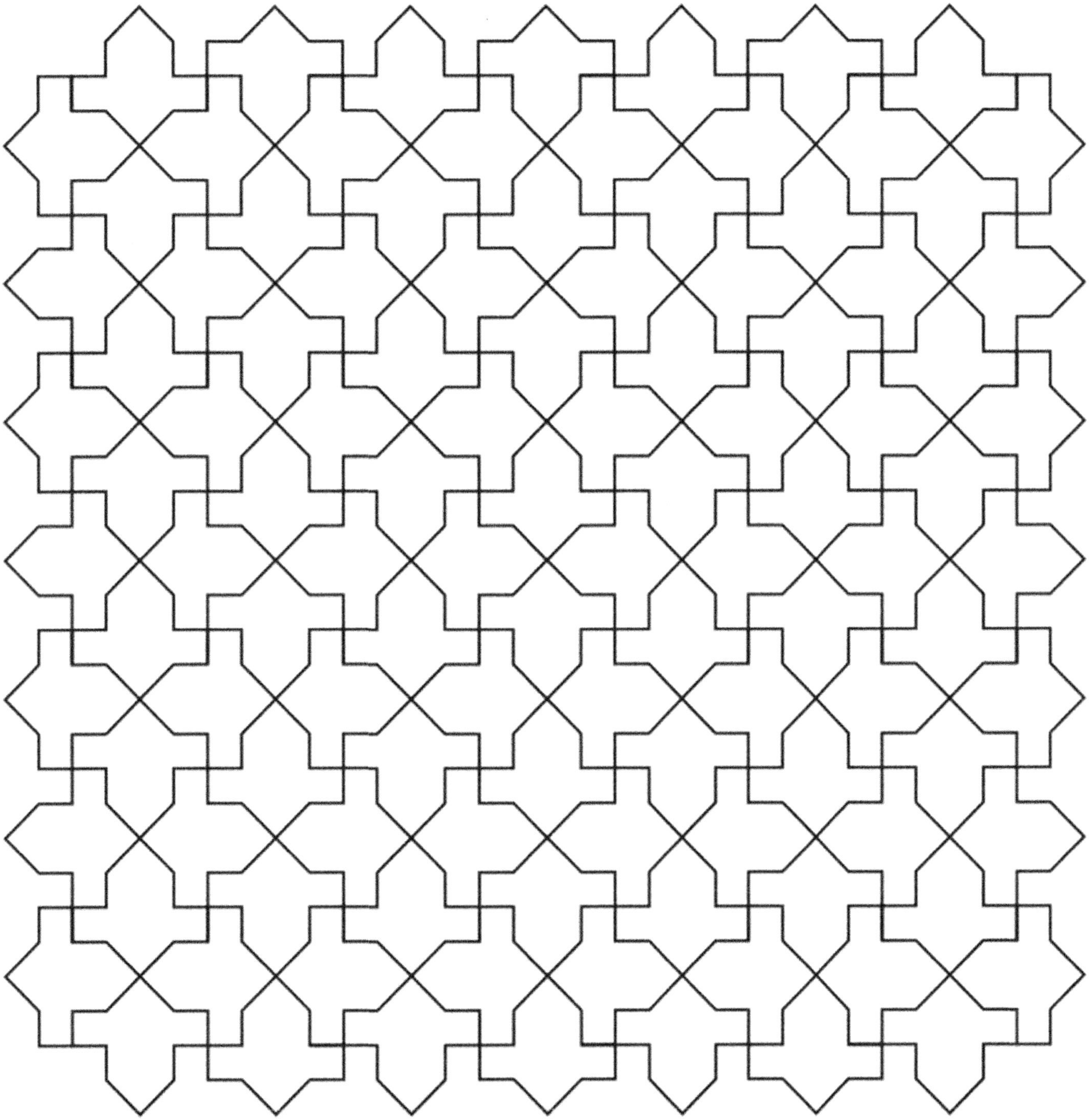

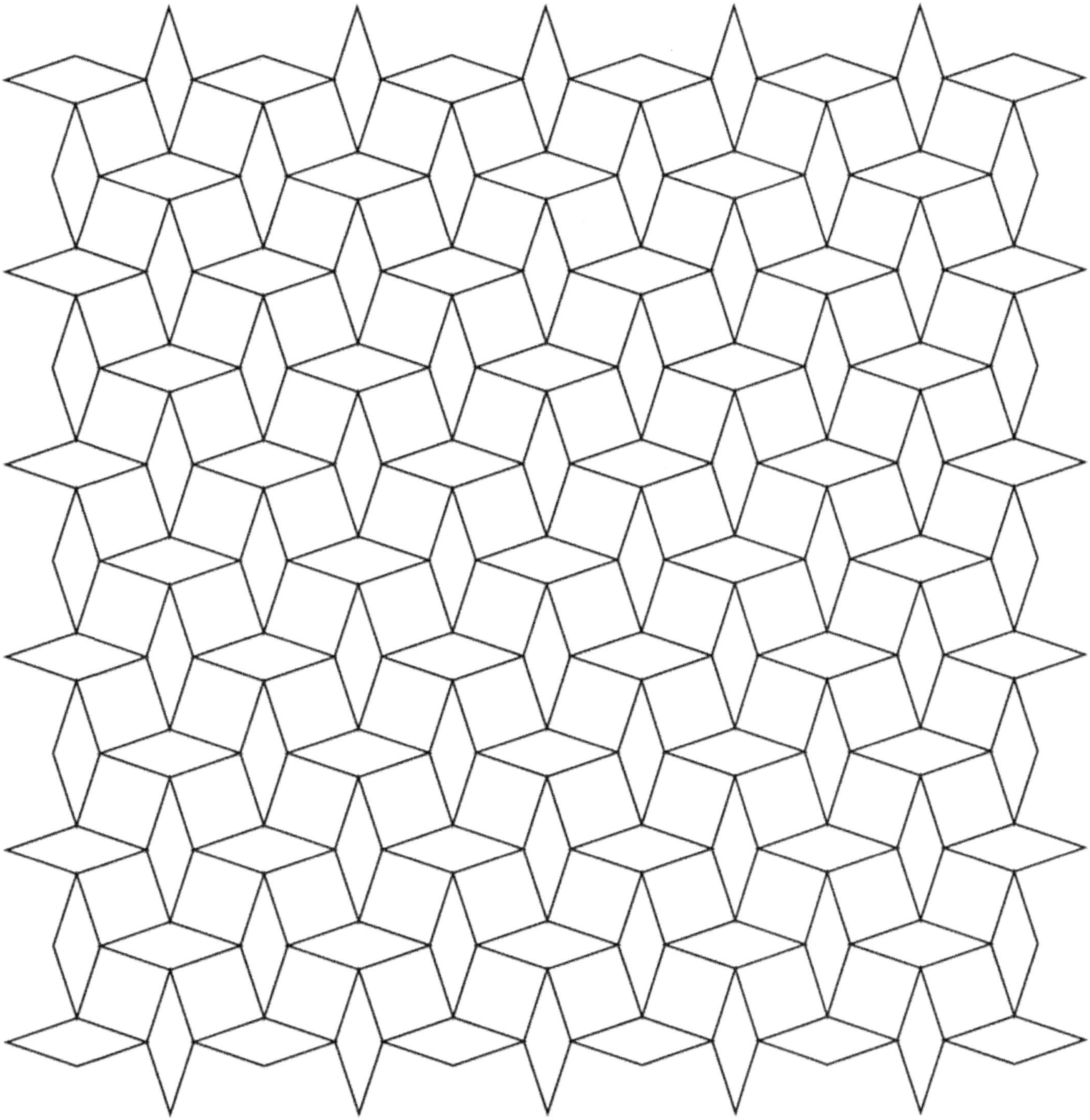

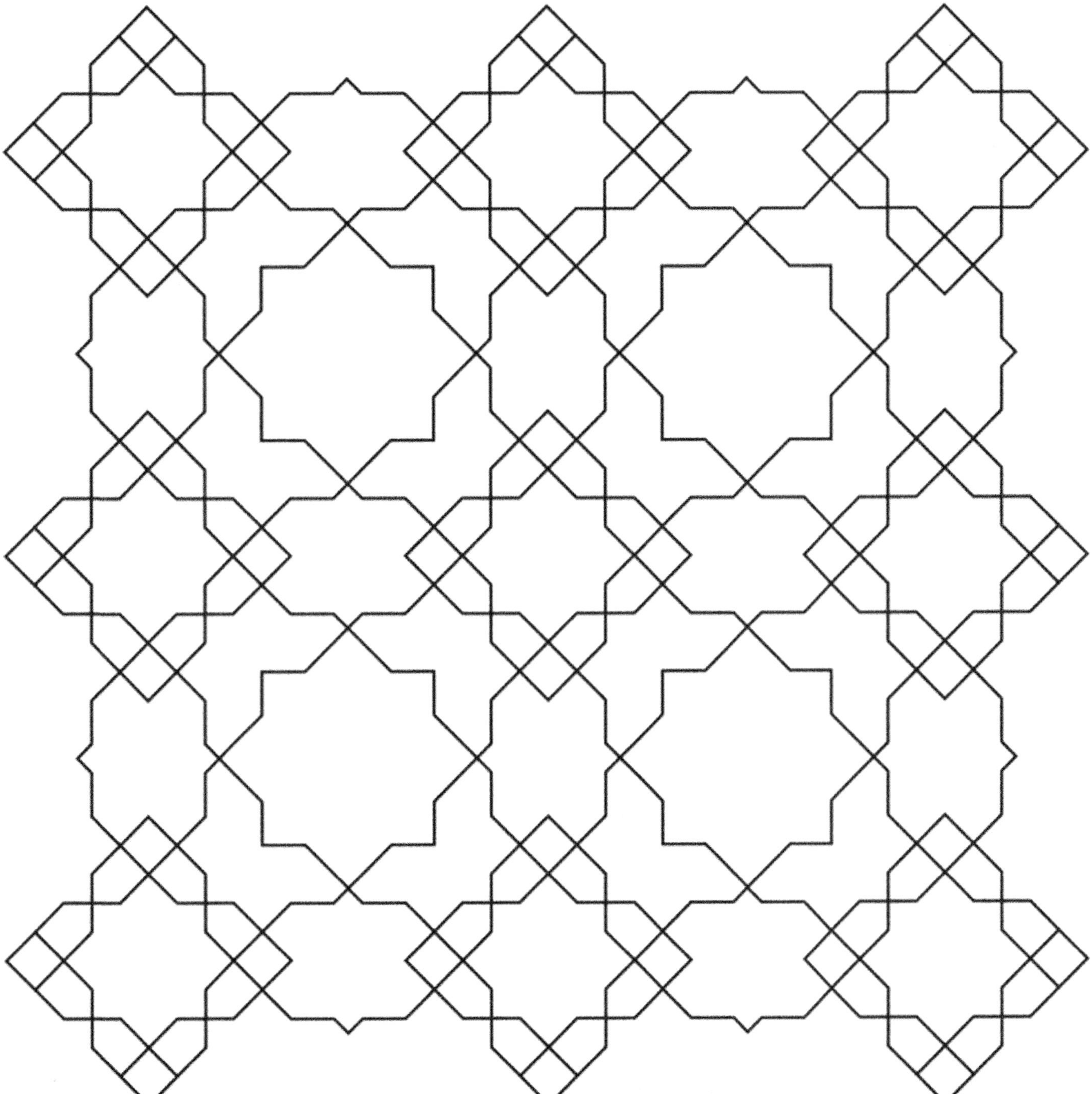

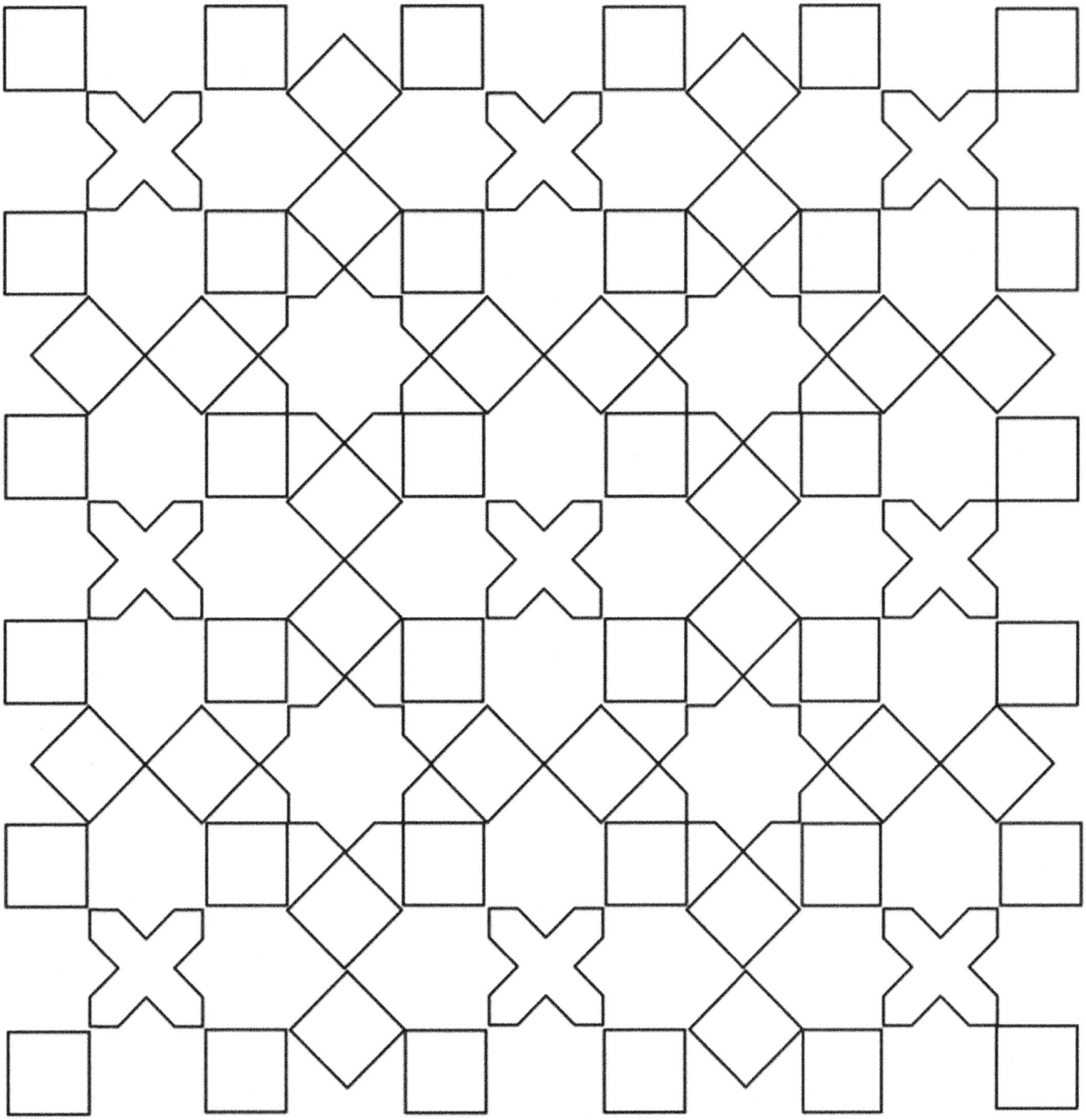

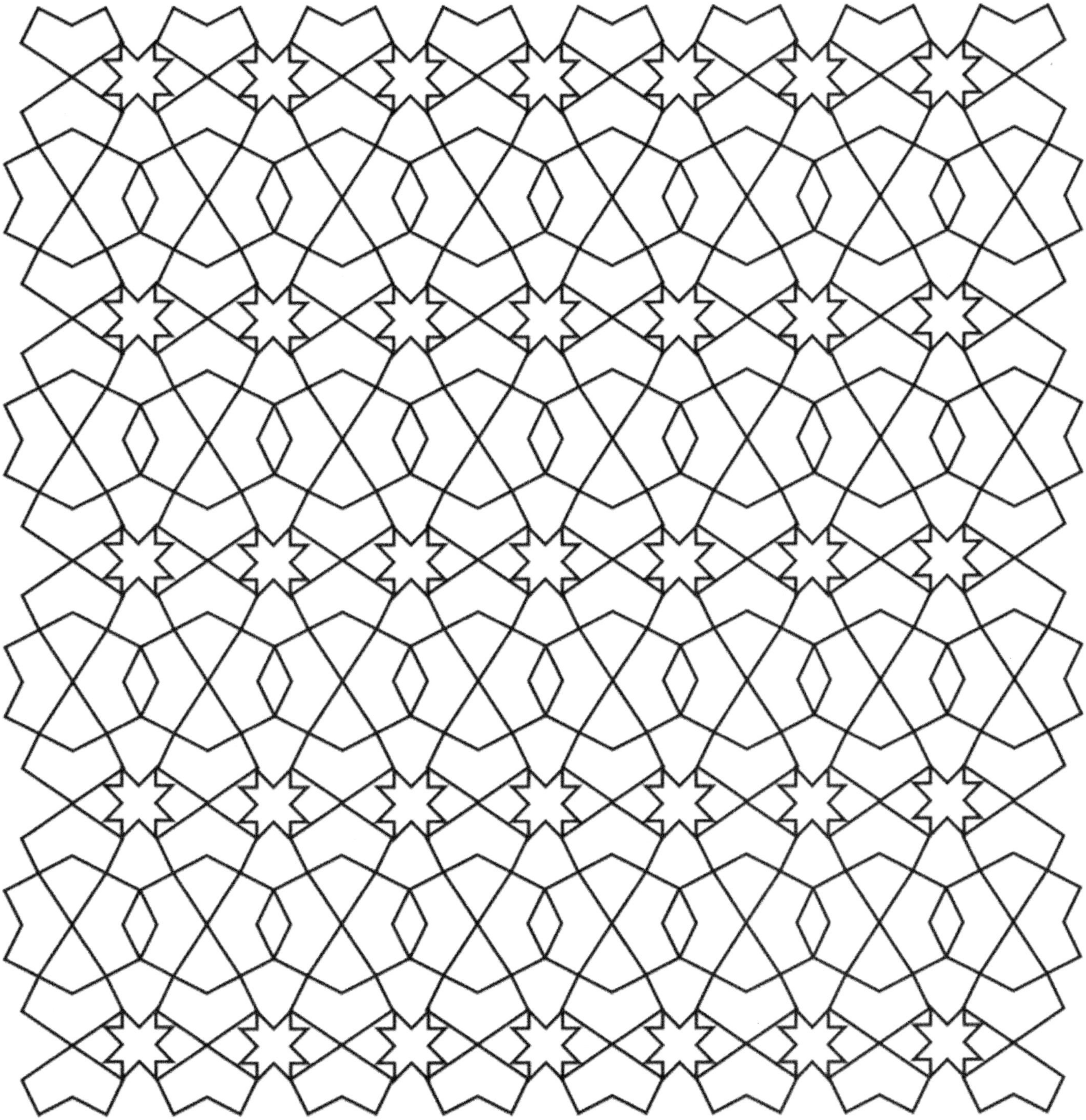

If you enjoyed the book,
please take a moment to write a review on Amazon.
Your feedback is greatly appreciated!

Printed in Great Britain
by Amazon

44151963R00064